I WANT TO RUN

....

THE OLYMPIC
DEVELOPMENTAL TRAINING
AND NUTRITIONAL GUIDE
FOR YOUNG & TEEN TRACK
RUNNERS AGES 10 TO 18

Written By Olympic Coach Sue Humphrey
Illustrated By Olympian Rachel McCoy

I WANT TO RUN TESTIMONIALS

"Sue Humphrey is the consummate teacher. Her patience with her athletes and attention to detail in all areas of coaching is amazing. One of the best to ever do it."

— **MIKE HOLLOWAY, HEAD USA MEN'S OLYMPIC COACH 2020, U OF FLORIDA HEAD TRACK & FIELD COACH**

"I have known Sue Humphrey for almost 40 years. Her expansive knowledge of the sport of Track and Field extends from the youth level to being the coach of an Olympic Gold Medalist. I highly recommend her book to anyone wanting to begin a running program."

— **ROSE MONDAY, CHAIR OF WOMEN'S TRACK & FIELD USA TRACK & FIELD, 2020 USA OLYMPIC HEAD WOMEN'S COACH**

"Sue Humphrey has worked with American record holders as well as beginning athletes. This wide range of coaching excellence provides her with unmatched insights and experiences from which great benefits accrue those she helps."

— BROOKS JOHNSON, USA TRACK & FIELD ELITE COACH, FORMER USA OLYMPIC COACH, HAS COACHED OLYMPIC ATHLETES SINCE 1960, FORMER HIGH-PERFORMANCE CHAIRMAN FOR USA TRACK & FIELD

"Coach Humphrey is a true pioneer and has been a great mentor, instructor, and coach. She has been a longtime advocate for athletes in sport and been the engineer of champions at the Olympic, World, National, NCAA, and State levels. She is truly one of the great minds in the world, regarding technique, implementation, and evolution of coaching and athlete performance."

— JEREMY H. FISCHER, LEAD COACH/ PROGRAM DIRECTOR CHULA VISTA ELITE TRAINING CENTER, USA TRACK & FIELD

"No one is better prepared to author this book of important points and tips for assisting athletes to reach their athletic potential. With a 40+ year coaching career which has included youth athletes to Olympic medalists, Sue Humphrey offers experienced coaching methodology while providing the intuitive knowledge that is acquired from real life experiences. Sue is a passionate coach who has made her lifelong work the athletic development and well-being of athletes of all ages and backgrounds."

— **TERRY CRAWFORD, HEAD OLYMPIC COACH, RETIRED DIRECTOR OF COACHING, USATF**

"Sue Humphrey is truly a World Class coach and an icon in Track and Field. Her ability to develop newcomers to elite athletes is remarkable using sound physiological and biomechanical progressions. Coach Humphrey's insights and training programs will be an asset to any coach at any level in our sport."

— LANCE HARTER, HEAD WOMEN'S TRACK & FIELD COACH, UNIVERSITY OF ARKANSAS-FAYETTEVILLE, COACH OF NCAA NATIONAL INDIVIDUAL & TEAM CHAMPIONS

"Coach Sue is a natural. She is values-centered and puts her heart and soul into being the best coach that she can be. Her overall wealth of knowledge and experience in the sport is second to none. Coach Sue has not only been an amazing coaching mentor with strategies and lessons she has provided, but she has also inspired and motivated me and other female coaches to reach for excellence."

— TONJA BUFORD-BAILEY, 2016 USATF COACH OF THE YEAR, 3-TIME OLYMPIAN, BRONZE MEDALIST 400 M HURDLES, UNIVERSITY OF ILLINOIS HALL OF FAME MEMBER, COLLEGE OF EDUCATION DISTINGUISHED ALUMNI

"I have known Sue Humphrey since 1988, and over the last 33 years I have known few who have the knowledge, patience, skill, and unadulterated love for the sport she exhibits every day. Sue has the rare ability to speak the language of the most grizzled veteran, as well as the young first timer in the sport. Sue is a track and field treasure."

— TONY VENEY, HEAD MEN & WOMEN'S TF/CC COACH, ANTELOPE VALLEY COLLEGE, CA, USA TRACK & FIELD MASTER COACH, USATF LEVEL I, II, III COACHES ED INSTRUCTOR

"Coach Sue has inspired youth to be Confident, Self-Driven, Focused and Goal-Oriented through the process that never ends. Everyone like her make a world of difference."

— DARRYL WOODSON, 2021 USA OLYMPIC SPRINT COACH

"Sue is a great coach that has worked with many Olympic level athletes. I have no doubt this book would be great for younger athletes looking to compete after high school, as well as parents and coaches looking to help them achieve their goals. "

— CHARLES AUSTIN, OLYMPIC GOLD MEDALIST IN HIGH JUMP, CURRENT OLYMPIC AND AMERICAN RECORD HOLDER, OWNER AND COACH AT SO HIGH FITNESS PERFORMANCE CENTER IN SAN MARCOS, TX, CREATED "THE TOTAL BODY BOARD" TRAINING DEVICE

"I have known Coach Sue Humphrey for some time as a coach who trains athletes of various levels in several events. As a coach, I have attended training sessions in which she has been an instructor and learned a great deal. Coach Humphrey has always been a knowledgeable and giving coach. All the athletes that have had the opportunity to train under Coach Humphrey have shown significant improvement. As a track coach myself, I trust Coach Humphrey's knowledge and expertise to train my daughter and athlete in high jump. Over a 1-year period of training with Coach Humphrey, my daughter has shown tremendous improvement in the high jump and recently finished as the #2 ranked High jumper in the USA for the 14 & Under division."

— **FRANK WILSON, AAU CLUB COACH, LEANDER SPARTANS TC, LEANDER, TX**

"Sue Humphrey is one of the best coaches the US has ever had—she's coached effectively at all levels, from age-group to Olympic Champions. Any athlete, coach or parent at any level would be wise to study and apply Sue's concepts from this book."

— **RALPH LINDEMAN, HEAD TRACK & FIELD COACH UNITED STATE AIR FORCE ACADEMY, FORMER USA OLYMPIC TEAM STAFF MEMBER**

"Having Sue on the track is an amazing experience! She is very encouraging when I need it and reassuring when things don't go as well. She is a very kindhearted person who wants nothing but the best for her athletes and I love it!"

— **ASHLEY SPENCER, USA OLYMPIAN, BRONZE MEDALIST IN 400-METER HURDLES, WORLD CHAMPIONSHIP RELAY GOLD MEDALIST**

CONTENTS

Author Forward   17

I WANT TO RUN   19
WHAT IS TRACK?   23
WHO CAN RUN?   33
WHY RUN TRACK?   37

TRACK EVENTS

SPRINTS   45
100-Meter Dash   45
Training For the 100-Meter Dash   46
200-Meter Dash   51
Training For the 200-Meter Dash   52
400-Meter Dash   53
Training For the 400-Meter Race   55

RUNNING   57
800-Meter Run   57
Training For the 800-Meter Race   59
1500-/1600-Meter Run   60
Training For the 1500-/1600-Meter Race   61
3000-/3200-Meter Run   62
Training For the 3000-/3200-Meter Race   64

RELAYS   66
400-Meter Relay   66
Training For the 400-Meter Relay   69
800-Meter Relay   71
1600-Meter Relay   72

Training For the 1600-Meter Relay	74
3200-Meter Relay	74
Training For the 3200-Meter Relay	75
Other Relays	76
HURDLES	77
80-/100-/110-Meter Hurdles	77
Training For the 80-/100-/110-Meter Hurdles	80
Lead Leg Drills	81
Trail Leg Drill	83
Starting Drills	85
200-/300-/400-Meter Hurdles	86
Training For the 200-/300-/400-meter Intermediate Hurdles	87
A FUTURE IN TRACK	88
Middle School/Junior High/High School	89
Junior College-College-University	91
Professionals and Olympians	93
DON'T FORGET THESE AREAS	96
Warm Up and Warm Down	96
Nutrition	99
Rest and Sleep	105
So Why Track?	107

© Copyright Sue Humphrey 2021 All rights reserved.

The content contained within this book may not be reproduced, duplicated or transmitted without direct written permission from the author or the publisher. Under no circumstances will any blame or legal responsibility be held against the publisher, or author, for any damages, reparation, or monetary loss due to the information contained within this book; either directly or indirectly. Legal Notice: This book is copyright protected.

This book is only for personal use. You cannot amend, distribute, sell, use, quote or paraphrase any part, or the content within this book, without the consent of the author or publisher. Disclaimer Notice: Please note the information contained within this document is for educational and entertainment purposes only. All effort has been executed to present accurate, up to date, and reliable, complete information. No warranties of any kind are declared or implied. Readers acknowledge that the author is not engaging in the rendering of legal, financial, medical or professional advice.

SPECIAL BONUS!

Want This Bonus Book for free?

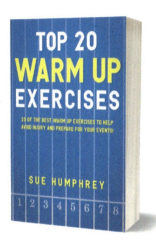

Get <u>FREE</u>, unlimited access to it and all of my new books by joining my book list!

SCAN W/ YOUR CAMERA TO JOIN!

AUTHOR FORWARD

Who is Sue Humphrey?

Humphrey was the Head Women's USA Olympic Track & Field Coach in 2004. She has served on two other USA Women's Olympic Track & Field staffs as an Assistant Coach and the Head Manager.

Humphrey started her coaching career in Phoenix, AZ, as an age group team coach for young girls ages 6-16. After running a successful national program in the Phoenix area, she became the first women's track & field coach for Arizona State University when Title IX programs entered the collegiate scene. She has also coached at California State University-Long Beach and The University of Texas working with both men's and women's teams. Currently, she gives private lessons to student-athletes ages 10-19 and coaches professional athletes.

Humphrey's experience on the club and collegiate scene led to her service for USA Track & Field (USATF) and the Amateur Athletic Union (AAU). In addition to her Olympic duties, she has coached at the World Championships, Junior World Championships, Pan-American Games, and USA Dual Meets with the USSR (Russia), Germany, Japan, and Romania.

When it comes to personal coaching, Humphrey guided the career of 1996 Olympic High Jump Champion, Charles Austin. She also was the first NIKE Coach of the Year and is the only female coach to have trained NCAA Champions in the High Jump, Long Jump, and Triple Jump.

Bottom line, Sue Humphrey knows track & field like the back of her hand and is passionate about coaching young athletes to success.

In, "I Want To Run," you will find everything Humphrey has learned over her extensive years of coaching Track and Field put into one, convenient and valuable handbook to reference for years to come.

I WANT TO RUN

"Wanna race?" What is more normal than kids racing on the playground or around the neighborhood? Who is the fastest kid on the block? Speed has governed mankind since the beginning of time. The fastest hunters led the charge to get food and track their prey.

Fast forward to elementary school playgrounds where kids were heard challenging peers and betting their lunch money during recess to see who the "fastest kid" in the grade was. Physical education teachers/coaches scouted the students who were quick for the school teams. We have grown up knowing that speed matters!

How many of us heard the painful cry of "You run like a girl!"? In our pre-teen years, this was the worst thing you could say to a boy. However, as women's sports increased in accessibility and popularity, that comment can now be taken as a compliment! Girls and women programs blossomed in the mid 1970's. Female athletes now are just as skilled as most males in their overall performances.

Why is running fun? The feeling of wind rushing by your face and getting from one place to another before someone else is a rush! Playing games is a foundation of our youth, yet it is through these games that we learn the skills needed to succeed in sports. Speed is a main component of most games, just as it is for most sports. With physical activity rapidly losing its emphasis in society today, we must now create situations for our youth to play and use their speed. Kids make up activities that involve competition with little direction. "How quickly can you get to the cones and come back?" or "I bet I can get to the fence before you" are familiar challenges. So, how do you get there first? What can you do to be fast? Can speed be taught?

Speed is defined as "the rate at which someone or something is able to move or operate." Speed means to move quickly. To be good in track races, an athlete can practice rapid movements repeatedly and get stronger while moving fast. It also helps if your parents passed along good genetics which give you coordination. Scientists say humans can run up to 30 miles per hour. Horses sprint this fast too. However, the fastest human measured has been Jamaican Olympic champion sprinter, Usain Bolt. He ran up to 28 miles per hour! The fastest female ever recorded was Florence Griffith Joyner, USA Olympic 100m & 200m champion. She recorded close to 21.5 miles per hour. Jamaica's Elaine Thompson-Herah almost surpassed this record for women in the recent 2021 Olympics. Humans are not very quick when compared to a cheetah (70 miles per hour) or a falcon (242 miles per hour).

Let's find out how to be FAST!

WHAT IS TRACK?

Track and Field events date back as far as 776 B.C. in ancient Greece starting with the Olympics. In fact, the Olympics are one of the oldest sporting events still practiced today. Track derives from the name of the course in which athletes compete, hence the name track. The track itself is a 400-meter oval consisting of six to nine lanes. The running events take place on the track, all the way from short sprints to distance runs. However, the marathon (26.2 miles) is raced on the streets.

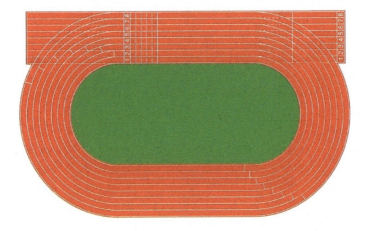

This sport has a rich history that spans many cultures, thousands of generations, and has survived countless wars. Some of the original track events from ancient Greece are still run today, such as the sprints and marathon. When one participates in a track meet, they are taking part in a rich history. These events have created legends and torn down the pride of dictators. The track has settled disputes between rivals and humbled the proud.

In fact, the marathon race began in a city named Marathon, Greece. History has recorded that in 490 B.C., Pheidippides, a soldier from Marathon, ran with news that they had won a battle over the Persians all the way from Marathon to Athens. So, when the first modern Olympics began in 1896, the race was recreated following the path that Pheidippides ran to share the news of victory. In the early 1900's, the overall race distance was standardized to 26.2 miles.

The ancient Olympic Games were created as athletic activities centered around religious ceremonies in Greece to honor Zeus and Hera, the supreme gods of Greek religion. Male athletes represented the various city-states of ancient Greece. Women were not allowed to compete; they could only watch. The various events competed at the Games ranged from boxing to wrestling to running. Winners received wreaths of olive branches and their local cities awarded them various riches and gifts. It was these riches which led to corruption among the winners and cities as time passed.

However, these Games were extremely popular with the citizens and held every four years, even though wars and changes in leadership took place. In fact, they lasted for over a thousand years before declining in popularity. The ancient Olympic Games ended in 393 A.D.

After over 1,500 years without the Games, there was a feeling that revival of the concept would be welcomed by the citizens of the world. A Frenchman, Pierre de Coubertin, believed that military training and skill development was vital for a person to be a good citizen. He presented a proposal to revive the Olympic Games before a meeting of nine countries in the early 1890's. The delegates at this convention were interested in resuming the concept of the Olympics and voted for de Coubertin to develop the plan. He created an international group to organize and host the updated version of the Games. This group is still called the International Olympic Committee (IOC) today. In deference to the ancient Greek games, Athens was chosen as the site of the 1896 Olympic Games.

Since 1896, the Olympics have been held every four years except in 1940 and 1944 when the world's politics led to wars across several continents. Then, the worldwide Covid pandemic of 2020 caused postponing the Tokyo Olympics until 2021.

If you have watched the Olympics, you will notice that not every race takes place on the same day. The Olympics take place over a two-week period with the track and field events the last week.

Competitions that you might compete in on the local and regional levels will be different. The runners will still be grouped by gender and age categories. Usually, athletes are separated into two-year age groups. Participation in track meets is not only for students in school programs. Runners of any age can compete in local, regional, national, and international races. Older age groups (ages 25 to 90+ years) have separate 5-year age group divisions in their master division meets.

Each track meet is a beautifully orchestrated event, and this is what makes it unique.

This sport will evaluate the individual and reveal his/her true self. What do you do when you fall? Do you stay down, or do you get back up? What do you do when your relay is behind? Do you take the baton and catch up to your competitor or do you settle for fifth place? These are questions you will ask yourself many times.

The sport of track separates the weak from the strong. We are not just talking physically but mentally. Those who have the spirit to press on make the best track athletes. These events leave no room for the athlete to hide; every person is in front of the crowd and is competing to the best of his/her ability. The best performers are the athletes who taste defeat, go home and train, and come back stronger and eager to try harder. Runners who push themselves so much to beat their opponents that they collapse just past the finish line will be the most successful eventually. It is the hurdler who tumbles half-way through the race, gets back up, and finishes the race with scraped knees and skinned elbows -- that is the real winner.

We will discuss the physical preparation for the various running events throughout this book. However, mental preparation is just as important, if not more so, than the physical preparation. Self-confidence is vital for all athletes. You will always find situations where you are disappointed; overcoming negative setbacks are part of life! If you always look for the reasons you are dealt a raw deal, it is said you view life as "the glass is half empty." If you try to find the positive reasons for life's situations, it is said you view life as "the glass is half full." As you get older, you will find that situations that seem so terrible when they happen will usually work out through time. The hardest part is continuing to move ahead and work toward your goals when it seems like too many obstacles are in the way.

The heartbeat of a track athlete is not just about winning but finishing and improving. Is this you? Then, track might be the right sport for you.

WHO CAN RUN?

The answer to that is simple. Track is for anyone who likes to run. For anyone who desires to sharpen his/her athletic skills and has a competitive spirit, track is a great fit. No one comes into this sport at his/her best; it is a developmental activity. Even most of the top Olympians were first introduced to the sport in middle school or high school. They started as newcomers, just like you. They became champions because they pushed themselves to new levels. They worked hard to become better athletes.

Running events are separated by gender. The sport is open to both male and female athletes who wish to compete. Typically, most middle schools around the nation have track programs as part of their athletic departments. However, there are organizations outside of school systems that facilitate track meets if your local school does not have a track program. However, most athletes will run their first meets in middle school via their school track program.

Most runners who start in elementary/junior high/middle school are between the ages of nine and fourteen. Many of these students have never set foot on a track, but everyone knows how to chase and run. Most youngsters probably do not have a clue to what their strengths are. You might excel in distance runs or sprinting; the only way to find out what you are skilled in is to try.

One of the ways to discover your running preference is to engage in practice exercises. Try running with the sprinter's group for a week or so and then try running with the distance runners. Once you have had a taste of both worlds, you can decide and pursue that course. You might find that you do not like sprinting as much as you thought you would. You enjoy running longer distances in which the pace is steady, or you can run fast, but only for shorter distances. The only way to know your strength is to try a variety of events. Hurdling might be the only exception to this rule. Hurdling is more of a sprinter's game, but it takes dedication to learn the perfect technique. The overall point is, if you do not know exactly what you are good at, there is no harm in trying everything.

It is important to note that you can join a track team or running club at any age. They have clubs for those as young as 5 years and as old as 90 years! However, it is equally important to find a qualified coach and/or group to train with. The athletes who began running in junior high/middle school have the advantage of experience over new high school runners. It is just as any other aspect of life; experience gives you an advantage. The longer you do something, the better you get at it.

Do not get discouraged if, at first, you fall behind the other runners. This sport can be unforgiving and frustrating, yet this is the very reason to stick with it. The act of racing, tasting victory, and learning how to deal with defeat builds character as youngsters mature. The lessons you learn will carry with you wherever life takes you. If you fail at first, get back up, dust off your shoes, and try again. This is because one day the warrior attitude you develop will pay off. This is an attitude that will help you not only on the track but in school, in your future employment, and other facets of your life.

This makes a great transition to our next topic: Why Run Track?

WHY RUN TRACK?

One of the most rewarding aspects of running track is the excitement of winning a race. This sport at its foundation is the most basic form of competition. The basic premise of this sport is simple -- the fastest person wins. So, when you win the race, you know without a doubt that you are the champion. How many other sports can make this claim? How many times have you heard someone blame a loss on the referee or an individual on the team? We hear this accusation in every game, but in track there is no room for blame. All runners come to the same starting mark and have the same finish line. There are no referees (in the traditional sense). It is just you against the other athletes.

The adrenaline rush (that butterflies-in-your-stomach feeling) experience of racing is incomparable! The excitement, nervousness, and eagerness all mix into the strong emotional pot, and they stew all the way up until the race. It is a difficult emotion to describe, but it is a character-building experience. Runners are forced to battle their fight-or-flight instinct rising their chest and tame it, as they settle into their starting position. Upon the sound of the gun, they bolt out of their stance and into the race. All those butterfly moments before are released and the race is on.

Racing is sort of a surreal experience; the mind seems to shut off and you just run. Every person is different but in the moments of the race, the world around you seems to fade. The only world that exists is comprised of you and the runners around you. It is in moments like these that you assess all your training, all your challenging work, and all your courage. A rival of yours springs ahead of you. How do you react? What move do you make? Do you have enough energy to pass them? All these questions are calculated as you race and most of them are answered by raw instincts. It is your job as an athlete to give your instincts the best body possible to work with. The stronger you are, the faster you will go. You only get stronger by training, and you only train if you have discipline.

You might notice that there is a lot more to running than you may have thought. This may be a surprise to you. The concept of running seems so simple. Yet, it requires much self-determination to be a champion. Although it is as straightforward as the fastest person wins, the real question is, how do you become the fastest? This is where the journey begins.

If you want a sport that will challenge you --that will push you to the max, that will make you stronger physically, mentally, and emotionally -- then track is for you. It is not a sport for someone who does not strive to excel.

Track is a sport that will get your body, soul, and mind in peak condition. It is the sport of undisputed champions. Finally, and most importantly, it is a sport in which some of the most legendary runners are remembered not just for winning, but for finishing.

Let's find out how to be FAST!

TRACK EVENTS

We will break down the track events into four subgroups: sprinting, running, relays, and hurdles. All of these are distinctive forms of racing. The dynamics of each event will be explained in detail along with some training tips on how to prepare for the event. It is important to note that the events listed are the most common events raced. Some states may participate in certain events, while others do not and vice versa. Let's get started!

SPRINTS

100-METER DASH

The 100-meter dash is the prime-time event of the sport. It is the event you imagine when you think of running. The Olympian who wins this race is crowned the fastest man or woman in the world. This event can be run in a matter of nine seconds by the fastest men or in 10 seconds by the fastest women in the world.

The event is run on a 100-meter straightaway of the track. It is one of the only events in track that does not consist of curves. The runners are assigned to a single lane, and they must stay in that lane during the entire race. To be successful in this event, you need to be quick off the blocks and have a short burst of intense speed. If you feel that you excel in sprinting, then this is the event for you.

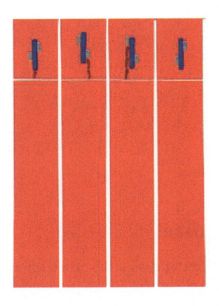

TRAINING FOR THE 100-METER DASH

Like all the sprinting events, you will begin your training by learning how to start. Mastering your start is crucial to success. Depending on your age and/or ability, you will use starting blocks. It is important to practice with blocks often before your races. You will want to use starting blocks as an aid to push you forward when the starter's gun goes off.

Starting blocks are two metal blocks placed on a sliding bar (base) where the runners place their feet, when they are in a sprinter's stance. When the official calls the runners to their marks, the athletes position their feet on these blocks. The base of the blocks is set back from the starting line by one shoe distance. Before the race, the coach will help you decide which is your power leg (the one that goes in the front block), and which one is the speed leg (the one that goes in the back block). A rule of thumb is to pretend you are kicking a ball. The leg you swing to kick the ball will be your speed leg and go in the back block. The back block is roughly three shoe lengths from starting line. The leg left on the ground when you kick will be your power leg and go in the front block, which is roughly two shoe lengths from the starting line. When you are just beginning to use blocks have the tip of your shoe in contact with the track and the rest of the foot on the pedal. As you get more experienced, your coach might adjust your foot placement on the pedals. Set your blocks in the center of your lane.

When the gun fires, you want to aggressively push against both blocks and drive your arms forward and backward quickly. Try to keep your head down and run as far as you can looking down at the track in front of you. When you get about 30-meters down the track, gradually start looking up at the finish line. Keep pumping your arms quickly and pushing against the track with each stride.

Have your coach/parent help you practice starting by getting ready at the starting line and having him/her give you the commands, "Runners to your mark, Set (wait about two seconds), and Go." Sprint for 20-meters as fast as you can and then come back to your starting line. It is a creative idea to put a cone or marker at the 20-meter line, so you know when to slow down and stop. Always run fast past the finish line of any interval you run. Once you pass the finish, gradually slow down so you do not pull a muscle.

Following your starting repetitions, you will move onto your sprinting workouts. The 100-meter dash training consists of a variety of short, quick runs. The focus is on training your body to sprint at its highest level. Start with warm-up exercises to get your muscles loosened up. Then, your coach will have you do a series of repetitions of sprints ranging from 20-meters to 150-meters. Some days you will practice sprints using a combination of sprints less than 80-meters. Be sure to allow a few minutes rest between each interval. On alternate days, you will do longer intervals of 90-meters to 150-meters. Again, allow a few minutes rest between each effort.

When you finish your workout for the day, be sure to walk, skip, or jog at least 400-meters on the grass. This activity allows your muscles and breathing to return to your pre-practice condition.

200-METER DASH

The 200-meter dash is an exciting race. It begins in a stagger start format, with runners in their own lanes. It might appear that the runners in the outside lanes have a head-start, but they do not. The reason the sprinters are staggered is that the outside lanes of the track measure a longer distance around the track. To make the race distances fair, where everyone runs the same distance, officials stagger the runners' starts. The first lane will be the furthest back, and the outside lane (usually the 8th lane) will be up ahead. The race distance is halfway around the track.

At all levels, runners have trained to sprint the whole race at maximum speed. For a new runner, this might be challenging, but it can be accomplished with training. A race strategy is to run the first part of the race at 80% of your maximum effort, take a quick breath and instantly exhale as you enter the straightaway, and then run the rest of the race as fast as you can.

The athletes will begin this race at the beginning of the curve and finish with a straightaway toward the finish line. Also, in the 200-meter run, each runner has his/her own lane and must stay in it the whole race.

TRAINING FOR THE 200-METER DASH

200-meter runners will focus using their fast-twitch muscles (these muscle fibers are located throughout your body and help you move quickly) in training and racing. You will begin by working on your starts. A great sprinter needs to have an excellent start from his/her blocks. With repetitive starting exercises, you will master staying low and exploding from the blocks. As you did in the 100-meter training, practice starting with a coach/parent to get used to starting with race commands. In an actual race, you must wait until the official shoots the starting pistol to begin. If you start before the "Go" command, you will be disqualified from that race. (See the 100-meter section for directions on how to use starting blocks.)

Following your starting drills, you will move onto your workout -- warm-up sprints, runs of varying distances from 60-meters to 300-meters, and cool down running after the main workout. Alternate short sprint days of intervals less than 80-meters with longer interval days ranging from 90-meters to 300-meters. Be sure to allow a few minutes rest between each effort as you did in the 100-meter training. This will let your energy levels recharge, so you can do your best during each effort.

Be sure to include running the repetitions on the curve and on the straightaway. One of the best ways to become a great sprinter is to really dedicate yourself to your training. You will run many, many miles overall in preparation for an event that will end in a matter of seconds.

400-METER DASH

The 400-meter dash is the longest sprinting event in track. It is one of the most challenging races in the sprinting category. Professional athletes can sprint this whole race, which is expected of them. However, at lower levels like junior high, middle school, and high school, sprinting the whole race is not likely. For younger athletes, they will run this race by pacing themselves.

The race begins in a stagger start format, just like the 200-meter dash, with runners in their own lane. There will be starting blocks to help sprinters get a strong start. (See the 100-meter section for directions on how to set your starting blocks.) Runners will race around the track one time to complete the race. At younger levels, most coaches recommend running the race in an ascending format of energy use. For example, in the first 100-meters of the race, you will sprint at 75% of your capacity. Down the back stretch, you should maintain your position and speed. Then, increase the next 100-meters around the curve to about 80% of your maximum effort. Finish the last 100-meters as fast as you can. You do not want to exhaust yourself in the first 200-meters and end up jogging the rest of the race.

If you decide the 400-meter run is your race, start with the ascending technique. As you get older and more experienced, train your body to sprint more of the race.

TRAINING FOR THE 400-METER RACE

Because this race falls into the sprinting category, your workout will consist primarily of sprinting exercises and some over distance work. Starting techniques are crucial in the 400-meter race, just as they are in the 100-meters and 200-meter races. As mentioned earlier, every runner will be provided starting blocks and will stay in his/her lane.

During training, it is important to practice your first 20-meters out of these blocks. You will typically do several start practices during the week. Your workout will consist of warm-up drills, a variety of running distances ranging from 150-meter to 500-meters, and cool down runs. Again, you will want to practice on the curves, the straights, and a combination of the two.

A warm-up drill is a movement like running that will loosen up your muscles. When you first come to track practice, your muscles are just used to the walking, sitting, and standing that you have done during the day. Now, you need to get your muscles ready to run.

Following the warm-up, you will move onto the full workout. Here you will run various distances at different speeds based upon your coach's plan for the day. The distances would range from 60-meters to 600-meters during the season. Like the training for the other sprinting events, your workouts will alternate between shorter and longer interval days. The shorter interval days will include various repetitions of 250-meters and less. The longer interval days will range from 300- meters to 600-meters. Be sure to allow enough rest between repetitions to allow your muscles and breathing to recover before the next one.

A cool-down is the opposite of a warm-up exercise. Now, you must get your muscle temperature and breathing back to normal. Your coach will have you walk, skip, or jog slowly in the grass for a set distance. This will help your muscles return to their pre-workout state and help prevent tightness and soreness.

RUNNING

800-METER RUN

The 800-meter run falls into the mid-distance category. Most meets begin this race with the stagger start method allowing the runners to "break in" (compete for the inside lane) around the first curve. However, in some scenarios, meet directors will use a waterfall start for this race. Have your coach teach you both ways so you are prepared for either situation.

This race is comprised of two challenging laps around the track and is run with some strategy. It is not a full-out sprint, but at the same time, it is not a slow-paced long-distance run either. That is why it qualifies as a mid-distance race.

This race leaves little room for error when maneuvering for a position. You do not want to get caught behind a slower runner and then have to waste energy by moving around him/her. However, you do not necessarily want to be the pacesetter/leader either. Most successful mid-distance runners plan where they want to be at each curve of the track and when they will make a move to get toward the front of the race. With only two laps around the track, it leaves little time so your strategy should be planned out with the coach. Of course, you never know what will happen in a race, so you should practice various situations ahead of time. Be flexible and adaptable is the best advice.

TRAINING FOR THE 800-METER RACE

Because the event mixes distance and speed, it requires some cross training. Athletes who compete in this race must be able to sprint to make quick passes on the straightaways, as well as during their final kick on the last straightaway. They also need some of the endurance a long-distance runner has.

Coaches have diverse ways of training this distance and it depends on the athlete's ability and experiences. An effective way to train for the 800-meters is to practice with the distance runners on certain days and run with the 400-meter group on other days.

There are several training methods you can research but expect a mixture of 200-meter sprints to intervals of 500-to 900-meters when training for the 800-meters. You will also run longer distances in the off season or even run cross country in the fall.

Once a week, you will want to take a day to run segments of an 800-meter race to work on pacesetting and race modeling with other runners and your coach. Try to anticipate various race scenarios and how you would react to them when competing.

1500-/1600-METER RUN

The 1500/1600-meter run is a longer distance covering three and three-fourths laps to four laps of the track. The runners will gather at the starting line in a waterfall type fashion like other events. When the 1500-meter race starts, runners will be on the back straightaway of the track. All the runners rush to the inside lanes of the track which can get crowded. As a result, you should sprint out the first 50-meters to get a position in relation to the other runners. Athletes must be incredibly careful to watch for other racers and not to trip or be tripped at this point in the race. During the event, runners are expected to have at least a full stride in front or behind another runner before moving in front of them. If there is a collision, the runner who did not have enough room to move is usually disqualified.

Many athletes who compete in the 1600-meters will also compete in the 3200-meters. These two races are similar in race planning and in much of the training.

TRAINING FOR THE 1500-/1600-METER RACE

You will want to train your body for the mid- to long-distance running of the 1500-/1600-meter and 3000-/3200-meter runs. Since this race is half the distance of the 3000-/3200-meters, training intervals will differ. Intervals in this race naturally are shorter than the 3000-/3200-meter event; they range from the 300-meter to 1800-meter range. You might run in grass fields early in the season to protect your legs from the pounding running on the track gives. Closer to your meets, you will train on a track most of the time.

3000-/3200-METER RUN

The 3000-/3200-meter run is a long-distance race which is equivalent to two miles. It covers seven and three-fourths to eight laps around a standard track. All runners begin at the starting line in a waterfall position. Once the gun is fired, racers try to move toward the inside lanes. Having the inside lane is the advantage in longer distances, which is why you see long distance runners staying to the inside lanes during the race. Try not to pass another runner on the curve as you will be running further than the others. Stay to the inside lane(s) as much as is safely possible.

Long-distance running is about pacing yourself throughout the whole race and not exerting all your energy at one time. If you were to try to sprint the whole race, you will not make it one lap before using too much energy. Running long races is about training your body to run at a fast pace for an extended period. It means you will be running about 65 to 70 percent of your max speed over a longer distance, instead of running 100 percent of your max speed for a short distance.

Since you will be circling the track approximately eight times, it is important to have a strategy. Some runners like to hang back behind the leader until the last lap or two and then try to take the lead position. Others like to go out and lead the race from the start. There are several strategies you can discuss with your coach. If you find your strong point is distance running, then this is a perfect race for you.

TRAINING FOR THE 3000-/3200-METER RACE

The best way to train for long-distance runs is to use a variety of distances. Most long-distance runners will train themselves by simply running several miles every day. When they exert themselves, it prepares their bodies to run for lengthy periods without needing much rest.

Some athletes will also take days to do sprinting exercises. However, these sprinting distances might range from 300-meters to 800-meters! They will mix these intervals in during the week to help condition their muscles to kick in the sprinting mechanism for a last-lap push. However, the overall conditioning for a 3200-meter race is simply running longer intervals mixed in with continuous runs. You will have a day of a continuous run approximately 20-30 minutes.

Training can consist of running different intervals: 400-meters, 600-meters, 800-meters, or 1600-meters. Running different intervals help the runner develop stamina. There are several types of training methods that distance runners use to train their bodies. Your coach will help you discover the best ones for you.

RELAYS

Relays are some of the most entertaining races to watch and participate in. It takes individual events and adds a team element. Relays need every person in the event to run his/her fastest to give their team the best chance of winning.

400-METER RELAY

This event consists of four runners racing approximately 100-meters each for a total of 400- meters. The first "leg" or runner will start the race and sprint the first 100-meters, the second runner will take the baton, a 12-inch long, round aluminum tube, from the first runner and will run the next 100-meters where he/she passes the baton to the next runner, and so on. Just like the 400-meter event, teams must stay their designated lane while handing off a baton.

Typically, the best technique is for the 400-meter relay is to use a right-left-right-left method. This way the runners sprinting on the curve (1st and 3rd legs) have the baton in their right hand. It is important for these runners to run on the inside part of their lane, so the other runners (2nd and 4th legs) will sprint on the outside part of the lanes. They will then receive and pass the baton from their left hand. This method provides for the baton to move quickly and easily through the 30-meter relay zone.

During the race, the starter will begin with it in his/her right hand, pass it to the second runner's left hand. The second runner will then pass it to the third runner's right hand. The third runner will pass it to the fourth runner's ("the anchor") left hand where it will stay for the rest of the race. The first runner must stay to the inside half of the lane. Then, the second runner will run on the outside half of the lane. The third runner also runs on the inside half of the lane and the fourth runner stays to the outside half of the lane.

If, at any point, the baton falls to the track, the runner who dropped it must pick it up and hand it off. If this is not done, the team will be disqualified. Additionally, there are 30-meter handoff zones for each runner. If the handoff occurs outside of this zone, the team is disqualified. A handoff zone is marked in each lane by two triangles. One triangle signals the beginning of the passing zone and the second one marks the end of the passing zone. The baton must be handed to the next runner between these two triangles. Since the incoming runner will be sprinting coming into the passing zone, the outgoing runner must start running before getting the handoff. The incoming runner will shout "Stick" (or some other brief word) when he/she is ready to hand the baton to the outgoing runner. The outgoing runner extends his/her hand backward while running. The incoming runner's job is to put the baton in the hand of the outgoing sprinter. Each team must execute a flawless handoff with the baton to have the best chance of winning the race. When the race is done correctly, it looks like poetry in motion. To achieve this baton proficiency, athletes must practice together often!

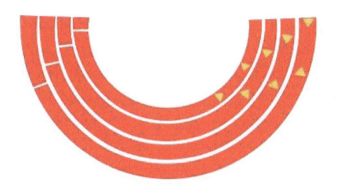

TRAINING FOR THE 400-METER RELAY

One of the most important parts of the race, other than speed, is the baton handoff. Just as sprinters practice their start, relay runners must practice their handoffs. Each member of the relay team should practice with one another often to reach the goal of a perfect handoff.

The handoff with the baton is planned out down to the number of steps taken by the one receiving and the mark of when to begin sprinting. When the approaching runner is coming in full speed, the outgoing runner must quickly start sprinting to get to the same speed at the point of hand off within the 30-meter passing zone.

There is a strategy for coaches to determine which athlete runs which position. Usually, coaches will select the best starter to be the first leg. This sprinter must use the starting blocks effectively and be able to run a curve well. The second runner needs to be able to receive and pass the baton well while running a straightaway. Some coaches will put the fastest or second fastest runner in this position. The third leg also runs a curve and must receive and pass the baton. This athlete needs to run well in pressure situations and stay calm when other runners are close to him/her. The final runner, the "anchor," is usually the runner who accelerates the best and runs well with the lead or needing to catch another team's runner. This athlete is extremely competitive!

Of all the relays, this is the most difficult handoff process; therefore, it must be practiced on a regular basis. It is important to practice both handing off and receiving the baton, as you never know which leg you will be asked to run.

The training for this relay will fall under the typical sprinter's workout regime mentioned in the sprints section.

800-METER RELAY

This is a fun relay run mostly in high school meets and selected relay carnivals. Each sprinter runs 200-meters. The runners have a longer stagger than those in the 400-meter relay. However, each runner must stay in his/her own lane for the entire race. Given the longer staggered start, it is sometimes difficult to see which team is in the lead until the last runner starts running.

Teams vary on the type of handoff used in this 4 x 200-meter relay. However, many teams will use a visual handoff like what is used in the 1600-meter relay. The visual handoff is when the outgoing runner is looking back to see how fast the incoming runner is coming to hand off the baton. The more experienced group of sprinters can use a blind exchange like the 400-meter relay, but they must put a lot of practice in during the week to perfect the handoff. The blind exchange is when the outgoing relay member is not looking at the baton. It is the job of the incoming runner to make the successful handoff. Practice is vital to this handoff's success.

1600-METER RELAY

Each of the four athletes on the relay team will run a 400-meter dash and hand the baton to the next runner who will run the next 400-meters to complete the 1600-meter relay. The first leg of runners must stay in their respective lanes; however, the second leg runners are able to cut into the first lane after the first curve. From this point, all runners will try to run in the inside lanes. This will be the shortest distance to the finish line.

The handoff during this event is just as important as the other relays. Typically, at the lower levels, the runner is coming in at a slower pace and the handoff is at an average speed. Yet, at the professional elite level, the runners are coming in very quickly! The handoff will be very swift. The runner who handed off the baton needs to get off the track quickly without interfering with other athletes.

At the beginner's level, the handoff process must be practiced often. Usually, coaches will have the outgoing runner facing the inside of the track to see where the other team's runners are. As your team's runner is coming toward you to hand off the baton, you would start out at a medium jog and look over your left shoulder with your left hand extended back for the baton. It is the job of the incoming runner to get you the baton. However, you must hold your hand steady and give a good target. Get the baton in your left hand and quickly change it to your right hand. While running your leg of the relay, you would have the baton in your right hand. This left-to-right hand off is used in this relay. It does not matter if the runners are right or left-handed. Then, as you are finishing your leg of the relay, you will look for your teammate's left hand extended and pass the baton to him/her. Once you pass the baton, get off the track as quickly as you can, but be careful not to run into another runner. The last runner (the anchor) can keep the baton in either hand since he/she does not hand it off.

TRAINING FOR THE 1600-METER RELAY

This race still consists of sprinters which means the training for this race will fall under a sprinter 400-meter training. Since this is a relay, handoff process must be practiced many times before the meet.

3200-METER RELAY

The longest relay (and most raced) in track events is the 3200-meter. Each runner will run 800 meters and pass the baton to his/her teammate. The handoff process in this race is much more casual but still crucial. Many teams, even experienced ones, can have blunders. A dropped baton will disqualify them from the race, so it is important to practice handoffs, even at a slower pace. Most coaches will use a handoff system like that used in the 1600-meter relay.

One of the more challenging aspects is the makeup of the relay team. Because this falls into a mid-distance race individually coaches sometimes pull from both the distance and sprinters groups. Coaches want to get the best four runners on the track to create a winning combination.

TRAINING FOR THE 3200-METER RELAY

When training for the 3200-meter relay, the handoff is important, because if you drop the baton your team could be disqualified. However, since the runners will be coming in at a much slower pace, the transition is not as difficult. One way to practice handoffs is to hand the baton between teammates as you are doing a warmup run. The training for this relay will follow the distance runner's training regimen. Coaches will give the runners various strategies to use during their 800-meter leg based upon the strength of the competition and of the individual.

OTHER RELAYS

Various relay meets might run different combinations of distances. There are several events which can be run using distances of 100-meters, 200-meters, 400-meters, 800-meters, and 1600-meters. A sprint medley might consist of 200-meter, 100-meter, 100-meter, and 400-meter legs or a combination of 400-meters, 200-meters, 200-meters, and 800-meters. A distance medley would be 800-meters, 400-meters, 1200-meters, and 1600-meters. There are even shuttle hurdle relays where athletes run back and forth covering the same 100-meter/110-meter hurdle distances they cover in their open events.

Relays are a fun way to create team spirit and develop bonding among a squad comprised of many individual event athletes. Most track meet schedules have a relay to start the competition and another one as the last event. The spectators and athletes get excited to start the racing!

HURDLES

80-/100-/110-METER HURDLES

The hurdles are certainly fun events to watch. The athletes who compete in the hurdles have a unique balance of speed, coordination, and flexibility. You could have the fastest sprinters run the hurdles and lose the race because they have poor hurdling technique. Likewise, a runner with a perfect hurdling technique could lose because of his/her lack of speed. Coaches will look for a blend of athlete who is a sprinter first and well-coordinated enough to learn the mechanics of hurdling.

You will notice that there are 80-meter, 100-meter, and 110-meter hurdles. This is because the girls run the distance of 100-meters at a lower height, the boys run the distance of 110-meters at a higher setting. This is the only event where the race distance changes per gender and age group. Some of the middle school and master athletes race at 80-meters.

One of the first things you will notice if you watch Olympic hurdlers is that they do not jump over the hurdles; they glide over them. This is exactly how the race is supposed to be run. As you develop your technique, every hurdler will learn not to jump over the hurdles but take a high, smooth step over them. The goal is to stay as low as possible as you cross over the hurdle. When watching a race of skilled athletes, you can barely tell they are hurdling, as they look like they are just sprinting.

Since there are barriers/hurdles in your lane during each hurdle race, you will need to have a more fearless attitude toward these events. It is important that you focus and work on your technique over the barriers often. This rhythm will allow you to have confidence. It is quite common for coaches to have you run exceptionally low hurdles when you are first learning them. As you gain experience, the hurdles can be raised a few inches at a time. Coaches will also push the hurdles closer together than the racing distances while you learn to use eight steps to the first hurdle and then three steps between hurdles.

The ideal technique of hurdling is called 3-stepping; this means you only take three steps between each hurdle. You will have the same lead leg (the leg that goes over the hurdle first) every time you step over a hurdle. Do not be discouraged if you cannot 3-step your first or even second year of running the hurdles. Some kids who start out in the hurdles begin by 4-stepping or even 5-stepping. It takes practice and sometimes your body just needs to mature a little before you are physically able to master this technique. The 3-stepping technique becomes more common on the high school level.

The hurdles are one of the most unique events and you do not know if you are good at them until you try.

TRAINING FOR THE 80-/100-/110-METER HURDLES

Hurdling is the only event where you will practice technique as much as you practice your running. It is common to spend a substantial portion of your practice time going through technique drills.

It is important to hurdle as much as possible. Also, the starting drills are crucial for this race, because in the hurdles every step must be accounted for. You must know exactly how many steps you take to your first hurdle and then each hurdle afterwards. It is the only race that you should know how many steps you have taken the whole race.

As far as the physical training, a hurdler's workout will fall into the sprinting category. Hurdlers, like the sprinters, will run warm-up sprints, full sprints, and cool down sprints. Much of your practicing should be done over hurdles. You can vary the heights of your practice hurdles and even moved the hurdles closer together to practice. The sooner you can take eight strides to the first hurdle and only three steps between the hurdles the better you will do in these events. (NOTE: some very elite hurdlers are now experimenting taking seven strides to the first barrier. However, it is not suggested for the young beginner hurdler.)

Below are a few training techniques for hurdlers.

LEAD LEG DRILLS

Using low hurdles (12"-28" high), the coach will line five hurdles up one meter (approximately three-feet) apart. First, practice marching or walking over the side of the low hurdle by lifting your lead leg knee first and stepping over the side of the barrier. As you approach the side of the hurdle, drive your lead leg's knee over the hurdle and drive your lower leg down to the track, so your foot lands under your hips. Once over the first hurdle, you will snap the leg back up over the next hurdle and back down, repeat this until you clear all the hurdles. It is particularly important that your lead leg stays in line with direction of your run down the track. The speed of this drill should start out slow or jogging and then get quicker as the drill is mastered.

For stationary drills, you can stand in place and practice driving your lead leg knee over the hurdle and back down. Once the lead leg touches the ground you drive it back up above the hurdle and repeat. This can be done with the hurdle facing a wall or fence. Then you drive your lead knee toward the wall/fence.

TRAIL LEG DRILL

The trail leg is the second leg that crosses over the hurdle. The cues are to keep the heel of your trail foot close to your butt as you pop over the hurdle. The knee of the leg bends up under your armpit while your foot stays close to your butt as you step over the hurdle. Another cue is to keep the toe of your foot flexed up to the sky. Once the hurdle is cleared, the trail leg takes a big step and quickly plants the foot down on the track. This is so you can resume your running action as soon as you clear the hurdle. When you aggressively bring the trail leg through, you will be able to run between the hurdles easier.

You can also do the stationary form of this drill by grabbing hold of something for balance. Then proceed to lift your trail leg up and over the hurdle snapping it down to the track. Repeat this motion several times. Practice on the side of the low hurdles jogging between the barriers.

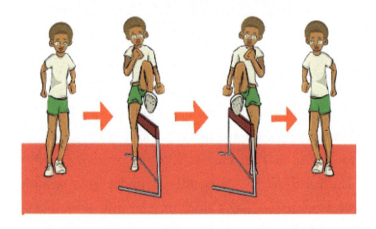

Beginners should practice and learn how to hurdle using both lead legs. Your coach will be able to see which leg you are more comfortable with as the lead leg after several practices. If you want to run the longer hurdle races, it is an advantage to be able to use either leg to clear the hurdle. This is called alternating.

STARTING DRILLS

Hurdles is an event that requires a flawless start. That is because you need to take the right number of steps to get to the first hurdle every time. If you mess up your steps to the first hurdle, it will slow you down, break your focus, and affect the rest of the race negatively. In the blocks, put your lead leg (the one that goes over the hurdle first) on the back pedal. Your trail leg (the one that goes over second) goes on the front pedal.

The best way to practice starts is to set your first hurdle up and practice coming out of the blocks and run over the first hurdle. Once you do a few successful starts over the first hurdle, add in the second and then the third hurdle(s) so you get the rhythm of running several hurdles in a row. You should take eight steps to the first hurdle and three steps between each one.

200-/300-/400-METER HURDLES

There is much debate among runners about which events are the most difficult races in track. Now, everyone has their own opinion, but if you ask a hurdler, they will tell you these races are not easy. This race is an all-out sprint for 200-/300-/400-meters with hurdles along the way!

Runners at younger levels typically begin running this race with a basic technique. Because this race is a longer race with hurdles, it can be exceedingly difficult to sprint the whole thing. So, many coaches teach younger runners to sprint at 75% to 80% for most of the race. This way the runner does not become quite as tired. However, this race is extremely challenging.

Like the 100-/110-meter hurdles each of the hurdler's steps are counted. The hurdles in this race are spread out much farther than they are in the shorter hurdling events. So, there is no 3-stepping technique in this race since the hurdles are spaced 35-meters apart! However, you do need to have each step down, so you do not end up stuttering over hurdles, which is very costly to your overall time. As you get older, the distances change from 200-meter to 300-meter and finally to the 400-meter race.

TRAINING FOR THE 200-/300-/400-METER INTERMEDIATE HURDLES

Just as you trained for the 100-/110-hurdles, you will train for the 200-,300-,400-meter hurdles. The only difference will be the distances. You will need to train with the 400-meter and 800-meter athletes to build up the stamina needed to complete this race. Even when you train with the sprinters, it is important to go over the hurdles as much as you can.

A FUTURE IN TRACK

MIDDLE SCHOOL/JUNIOR HIGH/HIGH SCHOOL

Depending on your interests and abilities, track meets can provide opportunities for you to travel and compete all over the country. There are school and club competitions through the various school divisions, USA Track & Field (USATF), and Amateur Athletic Union (AAU) bodies.

When you are just learning the different track events, you should try all of them to see what you like best! Some coaches/parents might want you to specialize when you start to show some talent in certain events. Try to keep doing many different events throughout elementary and middle school.

It is important to take note that your athletic career becomes more serious in high school. If you desire to compete at the next level, you will have to develop an impressive track resume. At this stage, the way to impress college scouts is with national and state-ranking times, and multiple state track meet performances.

This is the time to develop and focus on what you are good at. If you took the opportunity to begin running in middle school, then hopefully you have found an event or three that you feel comfortable running. During your high school career, it is important to try to beat your personal best every year. This means you should be much stronger and faster when you compare times from your freshman year to your senior year.

It is interesting to keep records of all your results. This way you can see your accomplishments. If you want to continue your track career in college, you will have a record of your performances to share with prospective college coaches. Even if you do not continue your track career past high school, you will have a nice record of your achievements.

This does not mean that athletes cannot try other events during their high school years, but at this level, each athlete should focus on a primary event or two/three. Typically, these are in the same categories, meaning you should not train to run a long-distance race and two sprint races. You can stick with the sprint events and add some hurdles or do long sprints and mid-distance.

JUNIOR COLLEGE-COLLEGE-UNIVERSITY

There are hundreds of colleges/universities across the nation seeking top-rated talent to compete for their track program. If you find yourself among the faster runners in your state, you will most likely have some colleges and universities reaching out to you.

Smaller schools typically will offer only academic or partial athletic scholarship aid. Larger universities will have more funding and can offer full athletic scholarships. Think of a scholarship as a form of payment; colleges will pay for your schooling and you agree to run for them and stay academically eligible. There are programs under the National Collegiate Athletic Association (NCAA), National Association of Intercollegiate Athletics (NAIA), and the National Junior College Athletic Association (NJCAA).

By now, student-athletes have found the race(s) they excel in. There are not many instances where runners will compete in events where they have not experienced some success. Most collegiate runners will stick solely to their primary events, such as sprints, middle or long distance, or hurdles. Every athlete at the collegiate level is so talented that if you don't specifically train for an event area, there would be too much of a skill gap with other student-athletes who have narrowed down their event choices.

During an athlete's college years, he/she will have the unique opportunity to travel the country and see unfamiliar places. Instead of track meets being hosted only in the state, they will compete throughout their region or conference. So, this means a college athlete will spend an adequate amount of time on the road traveling to their meets.

During an athlete's college years, they make the decision to keep competing after their college career or join the workforce. Some desire to keep competing and, from that point, they will attempt to become a professional athlete.

PROFESSIONALS AND OLYMPIANS

Only the best of the best earns the title "Olympian." Professional runners are the nation's elite. There is a difference between a professional runner and an Olympian. It is important to understand that just because you are a professional athlete, it does not mean you are an Olympian.

Professional athletes compete at national and international track meets. An athlete should enter many meets and record elite times to qualify for the Olympic Trials. If an athlete earns a spot by placing in the top three at these Trials, they have the honor of competing for their country at the Olympic Games.

Yet, most of a professional athlete's time consists of traveling around the nation and world competing in several events. At this level, it is the athlete's job to compete and keep their focus on training. Each day they strive to be the best runner they can be because they cannot afford to lose many races. Competing in track for a living is exciting, but it comes full of challenges. Athletes must stay in prime physical shape and work to perform better at every meet. Another challenge is that professional track athletes make money by winning certain meets all over the world and/or getting a yearly contract from an athletic sponsor. There is not a promised stream of funds coming to them. Budgeting is necessary! Yet, the result is extremely rewarding as one of the aspirations for every professional athlete is to gain a spot in the Olympic Games.

The Olympics is the Super Bowl of the track & field world. Every four years the best athletes from every country come together to compete. It is the most exciting athletic event the world has to offer! If you make it to this level, your dream has come true.

Years of training have all filtered down to a few moments. Elite runners have been training their whole lives and have only one shot to run their best race during this event. If they do not have the result they desired, they will have to re-earn a spot in the next Olympic games four years later -- talk about pressure!

Remember every Olympian started just like you.

DON'T FORGET THESE AREAS

WARM UP AND WARM DOWN

Taking care of your body is a major part of being an athlete at any age. If you are hurt or not in shape, you will not be able to do your best. Everyone will be at various stages of growth and skill levels. Coaches expect a variety of abilities when athletes first come to practice. It is what you do once you have started training that will determine your success.

Warming up is a critical part of every runner's day. Before you begin any practice or competition, you should do some type of dynamic activity. You want to raise your body temperature before putting it through a workout. Jog or skip around a field or track for a lap or at least 400 meters.

Then do a variety of exercises that require motion of your total body like jumping jacks, hip rotations, sit ups, etc. Get a routine that that includes at least ten exercises involving all parts of your body.

The perfect warm-up session should elevate your heart rate slightly and bring you to a light sweat. Anything past this point is too much. You will know when you reach that point by how your body responds, just keep a close eye on your heart rate. If you feel your chest beating hard or if you find yourself out of breath during the warm-up, slow down a little and give yourself a little more rest between exercises.

Remember, you should not attempt to train or run a race without doing some type of warm up. Many injuries happen because you are putting a lot of strain on your muscles, and they are not ready to be stretched that much. Your body needs time to ease into an activity. It is like getting into a cold pool; it is much less of a shock to slowly get in the water. When you jump into a cold pool all your muscles tense up at once. Likewise, if you were to attempt to train or race without warming up all your muscles will tense up. This type of activity can lead to injuries.

Recovery after a workout is an important part of being a runner at any level. Pushing your body to its max will come with consequences if you are not careful. Runners can find themselves with injuries, (muscle strains, shin splints, torn ligaments) that could have been prevented with proper care.

After every workout or race, you need to cool down or warm down. Once the activity is done take a short jog, walk, or skip around the track/field and do some light stretching. This will help your muscles from getting sore in the upcoming hours and days.

Since you used dynamic stretches before practice, you can use more traditional static stretches after practice. This is when you reach down and hold a stretch for a few seconds. It is not so active or dynamic like the stretches you used earlier.

NUTRITION

Food is the fuel your body uses. To be competitive, you must use the best fuel to power your body.

Watching what you eat is one of the top rules every athlete must follow. You will come to find out at the high school and collegiate level that many coaches will hand you a diet guide. In this guide, you will find a list of foods that are approved to eat and a list of foods that you should avoid.

Among the list of foods, your coaches will ask you to not eat will be foods high in sugar like:

- Soda
- Candy
- Junk Food

They will also ask you to not eat a lot of greasy food like:

- Fried food
- Fast food
- Chips
- Processed food

Poor nutrition makes it harder for your body to get in shape. If you have an unhealthy diet, it can affect your speed and stamina. Therefore, your coaches will give you a recommended list of healthy foods to eat. A diet of chips and soda will hurt your potential to be a good athlete. I know this type of food is easiest at lunch, but you would be better to pack yourself a healthy lunch the night before.

When you eat healthy food you not only feel better, but you perform better. Good nutrition is important in all aspects of your life, not just sports. Numerous studies show that when you eat healthy, you are not only helping your body but also your mind. Kids who eat a proper diet have an easier time focusing and end up doing better in school. As you get older, a healthy diet will reduce the likelihood of getting certain diseases. So why not just eat healthier?

There are numerous resources you can research to find a great diet, but here is a basic diet recommendation.

Among the recommended foods will be:

- Whole Grains
- Vegetables
- Fruits
- Certain kinds of pasta (in moderation)
- Juices (watch for high sugar content)
- Water (best drink)

When you feed your body healthy foods, you will run faster and be more consistent. This is not to say that you can never have unhealthy food while you are training. However, you should focus on doing your best to eat healthy while running and keep junk food in moderation.

If, during your training, you feel sluggish, you might try changing your diet. Healthy eating is one of the key factors, aside from track practice, which can impact your performance. It takes just as much dedication to follow a healthy diet as it does to train.

Healthy choices are something that every serious athlete must partake in to become the best they can be. Be sure to check with your parents and your doctor before making drastic changes to your meal choices.

Breakfast is a key meal for your day. So many times, you are running late, and you do not really take time to eat a balanced meal to fuel your body for the day. Grabbing chips and soda for a meal is like putting trash in your gas tank. It might run briefly, but quickly your energy levels fall. Plan to get up and allow enough time to get ready for school while leaving enough time to prepare and eat a good breakfast. Ask your parents before getting things out of the kitchen, and see if they will help you. Good choices would include a fruit, cereal, lean protein, and a low-fat dairy. For example, a bowl of fresh fruit, bowl of oatmeal with low-fat milk, and turkey bacon would be a good breakfast.

Hydrating with water during the day is especially important too. Most schools let students bring water bottles. Check with your school's rules before bringing water to school. Drinking fountains are not being used in most public places now due to the pandemic; however, people can fill water bottles and carry them.

During the school day, you do not have many healthy choices unless you bring your lunch. Some schools are providing healthier choices. You just need to know what to choose!  Beware of fried and fatty foods. A sandwich of whole wheat bread, lean proteins like chicken or turkey, lettuce and/or low-fat cheese would be a good start. A handful of nuts and fresh fruit would complete the meal with a drink. Beware of energy drinks and fruit juices as they usually are high in sugar. Check the labels and dilute them with water, if necessary.

Many athletes like a snack before practice. This will vary depending on the individual. You will not want to eat much, but some type of carbohydrate snack is an option. For example, peanut crackers, a banana, or some oatmeal are samples. Do not eat right before you practice; give your snack time to digest.

After practice, it is suggested to have up to 30 grams of protein 30-60 minutes after practice. This could be a protein shake (watch the sugar content), yogurt, protein bars, or a hard boiled egg. You want to be sure you parents watch over your snacks and meals to be sure you are eating a balanced diet.

Hopefully, your family has some sort of evening meal planned. However, with various work schedules, it might be up to you to get something to eat before going to bed. Your evening meal should have a balance of lean protein of fish, poultry, or beef and whole grains equaling half of your plate. The rest of the dinner plate should consist of fruits and vegetables. The more colorful your plate is the better choices you have made. Green vegetables are great choices.

Dessert is something to be limited. Assorted items can be eaten in moderation. Just watch the sugar content. Try to finish your meal by 8 pm and no late-night snacks!!

REST AND SLEEP

Athletes need at least eight full hours of sleep every night to perform at their best. Now, it is understandable that there might be some things that prevent a good night of rest, like a school project or travelling back from a track meet. However, if you are serious about becoming a great track athlete, you need to make yourself go to bed on time most evenings—even weekends and holidays!

Because the sport demands so much from you, your body needs rest to help recover. Not only sleeping but some physical rest is good, as well. This means after track practice, you do not go home every day and exert more energy, but you take a break and let your body recover. Instead of playing a pick-up basketball game after practice, you do homework, read a book, watch tv, or play video games. This is not to say you cannot have fun with your friends, because you can. But it is not good for you to overly exert yourself every day. Your body needs some time to rest.

Having the appropriate amount of sleep and rest will help you be ready for school and practice the next day. Not only will your muscles thank you, but your mind will as well.

SO WHY TRACK?

We have covered a lot in this book and given you much to think about. Track is one of the most competitive sports you can participate in. As you have discovered, there are a lot of different events you can choose. Since there is so much variety in the track events, everyone should find an event to enjoy.

Track is a sport that you can compete in or train for your whole life. As you get older and develop more physically, it is fun to see how much you have improved. Not only will you notice how much stronger and faster you have become, but how you have become a better athlete. Once you are out of school, you can still compete in track events at all levels. There are even national and international events for athletes of all ages. There is a group of people over 90 years old who still race! If you do not want to compete, you can become an official. Some officials are in their 80s and still working! You can become a coach. Most coaches are former athletes who entered the coaching profession and love it! If you do not want to spend a lot of time training or coaching, you can support the sport by being a fan.

Track is a lifetime sport as an athlete-an official-a coach-a fan.

One of the things you will learn as you compete in this sport is that sometimes determination can win races too. You might not always be the fastest, but you might have the most heart and sometimes that might just be enough.

On any given day, the best racers fall to those who want it more. A champion is not made in a day, but one can be broken in a day. You are only as fast as your legs will take you, but sometimes your heart can take you the rest of the way.

Remember to do your best and never give up. A champion is not always the one who comes home with the gold, but the one who finishes what they started. Run for gold but focus on crossing the finish line.

See you at the starting line-------

SPECIAL BONUS!

Want This Bonus Book for free?

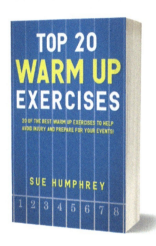

Get **FREE**, unlimited access to it and all of my new books by joining my book list!

SCAN W/ YOUR CAMERA TO JOIN!